Bright Ideas

Sunrooms & Conservatories

Tina Skinner

4880 Lower Valley Road, Atglen, PA 19310, USA

Acknowledgments

One need only read the rich resource guide at the back of the book to see who contributed to this project.

Front cover: Courtesy of Four Seasons Sunrooms, *right:* Courtesy of Greco Homes and Sunrooms , and *left:* Courtesy of Four Seasons Sunrooms
Back cover: Courtesy of Weather Shield Windows & Doors
Spine: Courtesy of Four Seasons Sunrooms
Title page: Courtesy of Four Seasons Sunrooms

Copyright © 2001 by Schiffer Publishing Ltd.
Library of Congress Catalog Card Number: 2001089994

Designed by Bonnie M. Hensley
Cover design by Bruce M. Waters
Type set in ZapfChan Bd BT/Aldine721 BT

ISBN: 0-7643-1418-1
Printed in China

Published by Schiffer Publishing Ltd.
4880 Lower Valley Road
Atglen, PA 19310
Phone: (610) 593-1777; Fax: (610) 593-2002
E-mail: Schifferbk@aol.com
Please visit our web site catalog at
www.schifferbooks.com

This book may be purchased from the publisher.
Include $3.95 for shipping. Please try your bookstore first.
We are always looking for people to write books on new and related subjects. If you have an idea for a book please contact us at the above address.
You may write for a free catalog.

In Europe, Schiffer books are distributed by
Bushwood Books
6 Marksbury Avenue
Kew Gardens
Surrey TW9 4JF England
Phone: 44 (0) 20-8392-8585; Fax: 44 (0) 20-8392-9876
E-mail: Bushwd@aol.com
Free postage in the UK. Europe: air mail at cost.

Contents

Courtesy of Four Seasons Sunrooms

Introduction

This is the book I wish we'd had a year ago when my husband and I began planning our sunroom. There was no book on the market then to help us explore our options for the structure and furnishings. I'm afraid that's obvious today when you look at the formal windows my husband picked out in contrast with the stucco walls and terra cotta tiles I chose. What we needed was a library of images to pour over together, to help us gauge our tastes and find the middle ground where they met.

These images can help you, however. Using this book, you can choose a style of sunroom, conservatory, or greenhouse that meets your lifestyle needs, and that works aesthetically for all the occupants as well as with the architecture of your home.

You'll want to get started with the logical first decisions: "What do you want your addition for?" It's very easy to imagine that you'll have a hot tub, a tropical rainforest's worth of blooming plants, plus a dining area AND comfy seating just off the kitchen. All of these uses might not, however, be compatible. For instance, if you're going into any serious form of botanical undertaking other than cacti, you'll find that the hot humid environment you'll be creating will not be compatible with your home's interior. You'll need to shut this extension off from the rest of the house. Likewise, if you're going to have a steaming hot tub or heated pool and you still want a view out all those plate glass windows, it's important to make sure that your room is properly ventilated. And if

you want to enjoy a hardwood floor or fine furniture on the new addition, it's doubly important to make sure that you will be able to maintain an appropriate atmosphere.

When locating that new addition, most of us think simply of the back of the house – maybe covering an aging patio, enclosing an existing porch, or piling up on top of a deck. And these may be the perfect places. They may be situated perfectly for an easy flow from the main, dark interior rooms like the kitchen and living room to the sunny new addition. However, make sure you consider all your options. A walkout basement can suddenly become more habitable, both inside and out, when it feeds into a Florida room. Or the garage might offer the perfect launching point for a romantic little getaway off the master bedroom. Roofs can be cut away or raised, walls can be pushed out, even ceilings can give way to glass. These ideas are hard for most of us to visualize, so this book can help you envision a new look for your home.

Chances are, however, that you've already got the space picked out. What you are looking for are ideas for the kind of windows you want, the color you want the trim to be, and how you want to furnish this great new space. Herein is the stuff dreams are made of. Visualize yourself there, then visit your local contractor or one of the fine companies listed in this book, and make your dreams come true.

Adding Architecture

A simple sunroom wouldn't do for this duo-towered brick and glass structure. The central conservatory addition was designed to mimic the lantern-style of the original building.

A mahogany conservatory was custom fitted atop an old patio and garden wall. Working with the existing stone boundary, the new addition seems part and parcel of the classic home.

This modern look was created when a sunroom was built on an existing, reinforced deck. Inside the occupants enjoy a glorious view; below is convenient storage space for lawn furniture and equipment.

Courtesy of Four Seasons Sunrooms

A crown atop a garage, this lush rooftop getaway is architecturally stunning; an archway, pilasters, capitals, and classic crown molding create a Romanesque effect in this elegant conservatory.

Courtesy of Four Seasons Sunrooms

Courtesy of Four Seasons Sunrooms

A five-sided conservatory abuts this Victorian, and ties in to the interior in period style — via French doors framed in fancy stained glass and ornate wood moldings.

Bright New Additions

Courtesy of Four Seasons Sunrooms

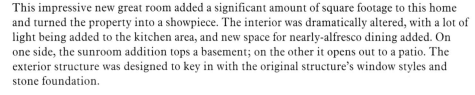

This impressive new great room added a significant amount of square footage to this home and turned the property into a showpiece. The interior was dramatically altered, with a lot of light being added to the kitchen area, and new space for nearly-alfresco dining added. On one side, the sunroom addition tops a basement; on the other it opens out to a patio. The exterior structure was designed to key in with the original structure's window styles and stone foundation.

Courtesy of Hartford Conservatories, Inc.

Generally, a new homeowner extends in stages, be it a deck, a patio, or a sunroom. These homeowners made a choice that will serve them year round, with plans for a ground-level patio to follow in another year's budget.

Built on top of an existing deck, reinforcements were added to support the weight of this solid mahogany and glass conservatory.

Courtesy of Hartford Conservatories, Inc.

A rock aggregate foundation was built
around this small conservatory, keying in
with the rest of the home.

This enormous conservatory would have made the original Victorian homeowners proud. The exotic mahogany wood and detailed craftsmanship are in keeping with the richly embellished tastes of the period, and the addition will allow the owners to garden year round – a passionate pursuit of our Victorian ancestors.

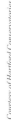

Courtesy of Hartford Conservatories, Inc.

While a brick foundation matches it to the home, this wood and glass conservatory provides a stark contrast. It adds natural light to the home where few windows afforded any, and adds views of both front and back yards.

Courtesy of Four Seasons Sunrooms

Dark trim and cedar siding unite this sunroom addition with a classic stone structure.

Two sunrooms were used to greatly expand the living space in this home, and also add a private, cozy courtyard to the back of the house.

Courtesy of Four Seasons Sunrooms

Courtesy of Four Seasons Sunrooms

This Tudor home was dark inside, while the backyard tended to be too sunny and hot to enjoy during most summer days. The owners chose a lean-to sunroom in bronze on the outside to match the wood trim of the home exterior, while inside hardwood floors and wood trim add an air of elegance to the addition. Diagonal floor planks make the room seem wider.

What was once a huge open deck is now also
home to a conservatory. As a result, the
homeowners have a new family room.

These Tennessee homeowners found that they rarely enjoyed their backyard because it was inaccessible: too hot and too insect plagued. By adding a 19-by-13-foot sunroom they created an "outdoor" living/ dining room.

Courtesy of Four Seasons Sunrooms

Matching wood siding ties this enclosed
porch to the rest of the home. Sliding screen
and glass panels make it an all-weather
center.

Backs of homes in most modern developments are largely ignored when adding adornments – no shutters or fancy trim. So this add-on sunroom really stands out and gives the back of the home some architectural interest.

Courtesy of Four Seasons Sunrooms

Courtesy of Four Seasons Sunrooms

These before and after pictures illustrate how glass panels were used to create a third story living area from an attic. The added space accommodates an inviting sitting area and a spare bedroom. The exposed roof truss and chimney bricks give the new space a charming country atmosphere. Doors along the back wall open to storage space under the rear eaves.

The back of a garage was lopped off, right up through the roofline, so the family could gain this fantastic sunroom space, slopped to mimic the original roofline and offer a soaring ceiling inside.

Indoor Greenhouses

Winter can be a long boring stretch for the avid gardener, but with a greenhouse or well-built sunroom, the plants come right on indoors and the blooms never cease. Here are some ideas for interiors and exteriors that should satisfy any green thumb in need of exercise.

Two pampered pets attests that this addition is
now the best room in the house to hang out.

Actually, this wooden conservatory is small in scale. Capping an old basement door, this little greenhouse room is a charming escape. River stones were used in the interior foundation walls to mirror the large garden rocks beyond. Note how the glass was beveled to create the impression of panes.

Courtesy of Hartford Conservatories, Inc.

This addition to an old farmhouse is filled with tropical plants, and is even home to a parrot.

With a sunroom addition, this family now
dines in a tropical getaway.

Courtesy of Four Seasons Sunrooms

A walkout basement now leads to a long
greenhouse/sunroom and from there into a
meandering garden.

These garden aficionados made their passion a year-round pursuit. Inside they've created a lush, tropical gathering place.

Courtesy of Four Seasons Sunrooms

41

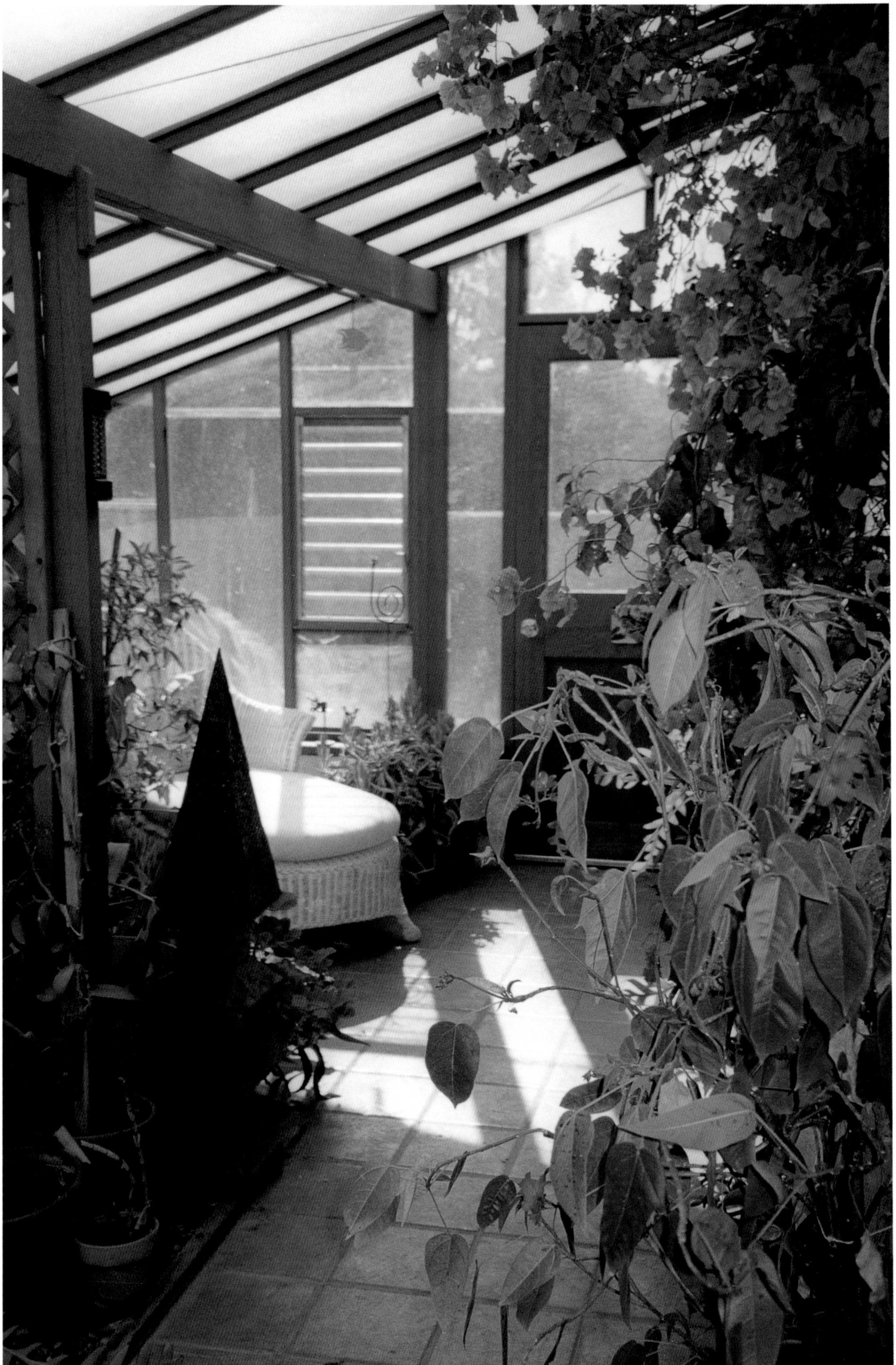
Courtesy of Sturdi-built Greenhouse Manufacturing Co.

Here's a wonderful retreat created by a gardener, complete with a comfy chaise lounge for those times when she wants to sit back and admire her work.

Oh the weather outside is frightful, . . . but inside the
temperature is just right for the plant inhabitants,
not to mention the gardener who otherwise might
spend the winter pining for a lost hobby.

Courtesy of Sturdi-built Greenhouse Manufacturing Co.

Courtesy of Sturdi-built Greenhouse Manufacturing Co.

Snowdrifts and icicles adorn the outside of this greenhouse. Inside plants are snug and protected.

Opposite page: Set apart from the home by a door, this greenhouse provides a tropical escape for the inhabitants.

Courtesy of Hartford Conservatories, Inc.

A panel under the roof of this conservatory mirrors
the post-and-beam construction of the house. Empty
in the summer, the homeowners use their new addition
as an inviting greenhouse during the winter months.

Crowning a raised patio, this comfy conservatory gives the owners of this historic home a bright place to congregate indoors. Clear-finished mahogany, beveled plate glass, and a wrought-iron roof crest give the addition its stamp of historical integrity.

Sash windows which open out from the
bottom, allow fresh air in even on a rainy
day. The technology was developed in
England, where it is a necessity.

Opposite page: This majestic room draws the
eye up. The conservatory addition was
designed to mimic the lantern-style of the
original building. A relaxed atmosphere was
created inside using natural wood rising
above a sectional sofa in soft, neutral tones.

Glass Houses

Here's a look at how great it can be to sit,
stand, and play in a room of wall-to-wall glass.

Glass Houses

Courtesy of Four Seasons Sunrooms

Wicker furnishings create the classic
sunroom atmosphere.

Cast iron corner brackets punctuate pane after pane of wonderful wood-framed glass, opening the view of a blue lake.

Courtesy of Four Seasons Sunrooms

Straight slices of glass panels create a bright
lean-to escape from the dark of indoors.

The Classic Conservatory

What is the difference between a sunroom and a conservatory? The answer to this riddle, in the industry, is the price tag. In truth, though both are sunrooms, a conservatory is defined by a classic English tradition wherein the avid gentleman farmer kept a conservatory for winter gardening. Since it is used for said purpose, a conservatory must therefore have a glass roof. These images were chosen because they fit the classic British mold for the genteel pursuit of indoor gardening.

An exotic garden room complete with central water fountain was added to the front of this elegant home. The open glass area is made private by a curtain of lush tropical foliage.

Courtesy of Four Seasons Sunrooms

A conservatory is underlined in white brick, making it a natural extension of the house.

An arched panel of glass above the entryway
creates a seamless transition from the
interior to a sparkly new conservatory
beyond. Formal rattan furnishings create a
showplace living room.

Adding on to an Italianate style home built over a century earlier, these homeowners opted to keep it simple. A dark finish on the aluminum structure makes the two-story building almost as invisible as its big glass panes. Inside, the conservatory has been lushly appointed with wicker furniture, brass lamps, and even a chandelier.

Lovely window inserts on the lower panes
create a charming scalloped effect.

Etched glass transoms are an eye-
catching accent below the roofline of
this lovely conservatory.

This Georgian conservatory addition was given a patina of age by the matching bricks used to tie the base wall to the historic home. The dark vinyl exterior color keys to the slate roof on the house.

A Wall of Light

Maybe an addition is out of the question in your home, but creating a wall of glass can offer the same bright effect. Here are some stunning examples

Floor-to-ceiling glass opens up a living room, commanding a view of river and mountain.

No panes, no curtains, no plants adulterate
this idyllic beachfront view.

An elegant, Japanese effect is created with
spare woodwork dividing up panels of glass
for this set of twin patio doors.

Courtesy of Weather Shield Windows & Doors

A small room was opened up and lit up by
French doors and windows that extend out
to the walls.

This stunning living room focuses on a
wall of windows arched to echo the
fireplace beneath.

When the weather doesn't permit life out on
the deck, the outside can still be enjoyed
through French doors and matching
window panels.

Cutting away walls and ceiling, and replacing them with glass impelled one family to shift their living quarters into the light.

Courtesy of Four Seasons Sunrooms

Lush ferns soften a wall of glass in this
sunroom add-on.

Patio Rooms

Courtesy of Four Seasons Sunrooms

A deck-top addition, this room was paved
in tile to create a classic patio room.

Gardeners and plant worshipers, these homeowners wanted to make sure that their passion for all things green and natural was fulfilled year round. Their indoor patio is a sanctuary, complete with a small fish pond/fountain focal point.

This indoor/outdoor room was simply attached to the home, capping an old outdoor patio. Ample windows on the existing wall extend indoor rooms to the new space via the view. A brick wall adds texture and charm to what has become a popular hot tub room adorned with tropical greenery.

Courtesy of Four Seasons Sunrooms

Courtesy of Sturdi-built Greenhouse Manufacturing Co.

This sheltered greenhouse/patio room serves as an indoor/outdoor retreat when the weather gets cold. Inside, plants remain lush. It is separate from the living areas of the home. Come spring, it's the perfect place start seedlings and begin the transition to outdoor gardening. Note that shade cloth is used over the area where plants are grown.

Courtesy of Four Seasons Sunrooms

A beautiful leaded-glass, arched transom graces the entryway to a stone-floored conservatory.

A small sunroom addition draws the kitchen outward, and adds space to the cooking area by placing the small family dining table where they can enjoy a meal on the patio year round. The new room allows the homeowners to better enjoy the fruits of their gardening labor, too, by increasing the view.

Florida Feeling

Courtesy of Four Seasons Sunrooms

Courtesy of Four Seasons Sunrooms

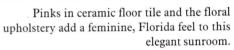

Pinks in ceramic floor tile and the floral upholstery add a feminine, Florida feel to this elegant sunroom.

Lace panels add privacy and softness to this summer room. A nice collection of rattan furnishings completes the tropical atmosphere.

Old world charm is evoked with wicker and
wood, set in a modern glass enclosure.

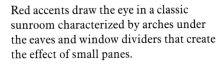

Red accents draw the eye in a classic sunroom characterized by arches under the eaves and window dividers that create the effect of small panes.

Courtesy of Four Seasons Sunrooms

The glass panels for this sunroom add-on were designed to blend with the original windows on the house. The new room is a transitional one between home and an inviting patio/swim area beyond.

Like plants, people find themselves
drawn to the brightest corners of a
home. Here two light walls of French
doors and ceiling-high window panels
mirror the grid of beams overhead in
this interesting blend of old and new,
and frame a favorite sitting area.

Furnishings make the room, in this case
giving the sunroom a formal flair.

Opposite page: Three walls of glass add light and ambience to a home office center, creating an inviting nook for some of life's less inviting tasks, like paying those bills.

Courtesy of Four Seasons Sunrooms

Wicker is the popular choice in sunroom furnishings. Here the sunroom was appointed like any other popular living space – table lamps, a cabinet, end tables and ottoman make this a comfortable hangout.

This Victorian conservatory is complete with dental molding, a crested finial across the top, and translucent polycarbonate roof. Built of solid mahogany, it is approximately 30 x 20 feet – an impressive extension of the home into the outdoors.

Courtesy of Hartford Conservatories, Inc.

A wall of this home was removed and replaced with glass, with another curving wall of glass and natural wood beyond. The kitchen and dining areas open out into a sunroom, furnished as the perfect place to relax and converse after a big meal.

Courtesy of Four Seasons Sunrooms

A formal look is achieved by creating the look of panels in this sunroom addition. Also, an added elegance is leant to the room by leaving the wooden room supports natural while the inside walls and window frames were finished in white.

Rattan furnishings underlie a flat-roofed
sun porch. The interior was finished in all
white, from floor to ceiling to add bright-
ness and make the room feel more spacious.

Bright upholstery adds floral accent to this sunroom. The homeowners elected for a solid roof with skylights to make the atmosphere a little more intimate.

Courtesy of Four Seasons Sunrooms

These homeowners have created a sunny room inside for cold weather outside, right next to a shady spot outside when the weather gets hot. A lacy swag between transom and generous glass panels pretties up this new family room.

A great room is made greater by two panels of glass flanking a
fieldstone chimney; a contrast in light and concrete.

Courtesy of Yankee Barn Homes/©Ross Chapple

An arched window adds architectural appeal
to this sunroom, made possible by a
cathedral ceiling dotted with skylights.

Courtesy of Yankee Barn Homes/© 2000 Suki Coughlin/Paula McFarland Stylist

Dark beams contrast with white wall panels
and crystal panes in this sunny, formally
furnished living room.

Courtesy of Yankee Barn Homes/© 2000 Suki Coughlin/Paula McFarland Stylist

A window seat is the ultimate way to soak in the sun indoors. Here an inviting window retreat underlines an enormous bank of bright windowpanes.

Light Fare

How's this for the perfect breakfast nook? A glass-roofed porch affords its occupants a fish-eye view, including an overlook of the Columbia River. A collection of cacti is shielded from Washington State's wet weather.

Courtesy of Greco Homes and Sunrooms

Courtesy of Greco Homes and Sunrooms

An arch of glass panels expands and brightens a kitchen area and adds seating room. Light lovers, these homeowners fit in glass wherever possible, including the space above the kitchen cabinets, under the eaves.

Opposite page: By arching out a wall of glass, this formal dining area came to command an appetizing view.

It almost feels like you're outside, even
before you pass through these elegant patio
doors with transoms to the screened porch
beyond.

Courtesy of Weather Shield Windows & Doors

A panel three-quarters of the way up breaks
up a wall of glass, underlined by a scalloped
curtain.

French doors and big panels of glass create
a patio room indoors. Cheerful curtain
panels on the transom windows add flair.

A semi-circle of round-top windows marks
the periphery of this elegant dining area.

Courtesy of Weather Shield Windows & Doors

Floor-to-ceiling windows wend
around a circular sunroom extension
of kitchen and dining areas.

A unique, lattice-like design was created
in timber and glass for this sunny
kitchen/dining room.

Courtesy of Four Seasons Sunrooms

Transom windows add style and draw light
in from a new sunroom/dining room.

Opposite page: Furnishings are everything.
Here a dining set creates a formal place to
eat.

From the kitchen inside, the family moves food under open sky (and a little glass) to dine, then they can clear and wash their dishes beside an unadulterated view of the yard.

Opposite page: A kitchen and dining area were widened by the addition of a sunroom.

A kitchen wall was sacrificed, but look at the view that was gained. Besides a view, the cook often enjoys additional company these days, with comfy seating and an attractive location luring family members into her domain.

Opposite page: A sunny nook invites family members to take their meals and play games together, under the almost-open sky.

Wicker furnishings and bright blue tiles give this breakfast nook its cheerful atmosphere.

Extending off the kitchen, this breakfast
nook was framed in glass.

There are no mystery dishes in this cook's
kitchen – light from wall and ceiling
illuminates her work.

A cavernous room like this needs a lot of light, and natural light is always best. So windows were installed floor to ceiling flanking the chimney and along the outer walls.

Step Right Outside

The whole reason we build sunrooms is because we really want to be outside. These rooms are as close as we can get when it is raining or some other worse form of precipitation. So these rooms are examples of simple transitions from sunny inside to sunny outdoors.

Rattan furnishings, lush plants, and natural wood interior make this sunroom addition a welcome hangout when it's too cool to be by the pool.

A few steps from the sunroom, a small
pond and a brick patio beckon.

Outdoor lovers, these homeowners created
an elaborate brick patio, complete with
stone furnishings. When the weather isn't
cooperating, however, they can retreat back
up the two sets of curving stairs to their
snug little conservatory.

A conservatory situated in the center of this home blends right in. it serves as portal to the pool and patio beyond.

A sunroom shares a starring role with a large hot tub in this private patio courtyard.

Courtesy of Four Seasons Sunrooms

A vast wooden deck sees heavy traffic in the summertime. When winter winds blow, however, the occupants move inside this two-story sunroom addition, and use the deck only as transit to a bubbling hot tub.

What was once a huge open deck is now also home to a conservatory. As a result, the homeowners have a new family room.

131

The back of this home revolves around a small patio, with both a sunroom and sliding glass doors off the family room leading to this outside haven. As the trees attest, though, it's fall and time to move activities behind glass.

Vantage Points

A sun wall
marries this
living area with
the maritime
environment of
Puget Sound
beyond.

Courtesy of Hartford Conservatories, Inc.

Why on a rooftop? All that sun and an enormous measure of privacy. This is a perfect way to capture a place in the sun, on a property where land space is limited.

134

Courtesy of Four Seasons Sunrooms

This family opened their home to the outdoors with an all-weather sunroom. It's only another step to the deck beyond, so there's always a connection with the forest just beyond their backyard.

With a screen porch below and a sunroom on top, the roof had to be kept fairly flat if it wasn't to rise above the home.

Courtesy of Four Seasons Sunrooms

Because these ranch house owners wanted such a big sunroom, a design consultant put two units that would normally back up to a house, back-to-back with each other. A base wall in matching brick marries the addition to the original house.

A large, screened-in area is all that's needed to enjoy most days in sunny Sarasota, Florida. When it is raining, however, the homeowners can retire to a second story Victorian conservatory for an unobstructed view.

Courtesy of Four Seasons Sunrooms

Courtesy of Four Seasons Sunrooms

See how these homeowners have opened up
their kitchen, creating light for the interior
of the home, and adding an inviting place to
eat under the open sky? Beyond that, when
the sky and insects are being agreeable,
there's alfresco dining on the deck.

Wrapping around the back of the house on an elevated deck, this sunroom addition became an instant hangout, offering sweeping views and furnished for all-weather comfort.

Courtesy of Four Seasons Sunrooms

146

What a perfect way to take in the waterfront view, from a second-story sunroom perched on what was once a single-season deck.

Mixed Uses

A sunroom enclosure brings luxury and
year-round aqua-enjoyment to these swim
enthusiasts. No more need for vacuuming
up fallen leaves, either.

An artist got an inspiring space to practice at the keys with this sunroom addition dedicated to the piano.

Swimming is considered one of the most perfect forms of exercise, especially for people whose bones or ligaments can't take the pressure of gravity while working to raise the heart rate. A sunroom enclosure can make it possible to enjoy the therapeutic benefits of water workouts all year.

Courtesy of Four Seasons Sunrooms

Courtesy of Four Seasons Sunrooms

These homeowners wanted a poolroom that would give one the impression of being outdoors, even when the weather wasn't agreeable. On the other side, however, they didn't want to alter the appearance of their traditional style home; thus the dual natures of one long poolroom connecting the main house with the garage.

In addition to a sunroom, these
homeowners wanted a covered walkway to
the garage.

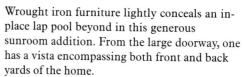

Wrought iron furniture lightly conceals an in-place lap pool beyond in this generous sunroom addition. From the large doorway, one has a vista encompassing both front and back yards of the home.

Courtesy of Four Seasons Sunrooms

Here's a wondrous way to awake – practi-
cally outside. For those mornings when the
owners don't want to rise with the sun,
they've installed curtains that easily slide
across the floor-to-ceiling windows and
doors.

Courtesy of Yankee Barn Homes/© 2000 Suki Coughlin/Paula McFarland Stylist

Glass walls on three sides of a master
bedroom make this a wonderful place to
wake up in the morning.

Courtesy of Yankee Barn Homes/© 2000 Saki Coughlin/Paula McFarland Stylist

Resource Guide

The following list represents those fine companies that contributed images for this book. They may have showrooms or representatives in your area. Your yellow pages are also a good resource for sunroom/conservatory providers and builders in your area. It's a good idea also to inquire with friends and neighbors who've installed sunrooms or conservatories – a personal recommendation is your best starting point when it comes to contractors and providers.

Four Seasons Sunrooms
5005 Veterans Memorial Highway
Holbrook, NY 11741
800-533-0887/Fax: 516-563-4010
www.FourSeasonsSunrooms.com
email: more info@four-seasons-sunrooms.com

Four Seasons Sunrooms designs, builds, and ships its exclusive product line to more than 300 independently owned and operated franchises and dealers in over thirty countries. Their sunrooms and skylights are designed to control both solar heat gain and winter heat loss in such extreme climates as Canada and Alaska and Arizona and the Middle East.

Greco Homes and Sunrooms
11403 58th Avenue East
Puyallup, WA 98373
800-933-7666/Fax: 253-848-7847
www.grecohomes.com

Designers and manufacturers of custom homes and sunrooms.

Hartford Conservatories, Inc.
96A Commerce Way
Woburn, MA 01801
781-937-9050/937-9025
hartford@hartford-con.com
www.hartford-con.com

Originally founded as a subsidiary of an English company, Hartford brought the British tradition of solid mahogany conservatories to the United States. The company now licenses showrooms and dealers across the country and supervises the sales and installation of its uniquely designed product, all of which comes with a lifetime guarantee.

Sturdi-built Greenhouse Manufacturing Co.
11304 S.W. Boones Ferry Road
Portland, OR 97219
800-722-4155
sturdi@ipns.com
www.sturdi-built.com

Sturdi-built is a 40-year-old family owned and operated business, manufacturing glass rooms that are perfect as a garden room, sun room, or spa enclosure. These units are designed for plant cultivation, and generally kept separate from main living areas by a door.

Weather Shield Windows & Doors
P.O. Box 309
Medford, WI 54451
800-477-6808
www.weathershield.com

One of the nation's largest window manufacturers, Weather Shield Windows & Doors is based in Medford, Wisconsin, and operates plants in Medford, Ladysmith, and Greenwood, Wisconsin and in Logan, Utah.

Yankee Barn Homes
131 Yankee Barn Road
Grantham, NH 03753
800-258-9786
www.yankeebarnhomes.com

Yankee Barn Homes works with customers to custom design homes using reclaimed timbers. Their homes are characterized by their New England barn style and an enormously flexible timber-frame system that allows for big windows with sweeping views and great rooms with cathedral ceilings.